MW00697752

This edition copyright © 2000 Lion Publishing

Published by
Lion Publishing plc
Sandy Lane West, Oxford, England
www.lion-publishing.co.uk
ISBN 0 7459 4556 2

First edition 2000
1 3 5 7 9 10 8 6 4 2 0

Music acknowledgments

℗ 2000 Classic Fox Records.
Recording under licence from Classic Fox Records Limited,
1 Collington Avenue, Bexhill-on-Sea, East Sussex TN39 3PX.

Picture acknowledgments

Cover illustration: detail taken from the Lindisfarne Gospels,
copyright © British Library, London/AKG London.

Text acknowledgments

Pages 12–13, 16–17, 24–25:
Joyce Denham, from *A Child's Book of Celtic Prayers*.

Every effort has been made to trace and acknowledge
copyright holders of all the quotations in this book.
We apologize for any errors or omissions that may remain,
and would ask those concerned to contact the publishers,
who will ensure that full acknowledgment is made in the future.

Spelling and punctuation of quotations may have been modernized.

A catalogue record for this book is available
from the British Library

Typeset in 15/22 Calligraphic 421
Printed and bound in Singapore

THE CELTIC SPIRIT

POEMS, PRAYERS & MUSIC

LION
Giftlines

the way

Alone with none but thee, my God,
I journey on my way.
What need I fear, when thou art near,
O King of night and day?
More safe am I within thy hand
Than if a host did round me stand.

St Columba of Iona

A low prayer, a high prayer,
I send through space.
Arrange them thyself,
O thou King of Grace.

FROM THE POEM-BOOK OF THE GAEL

Be thou my vision,
O Lord of my heart,
Be all else but naught to me,
Save that thou art;
Be thou my best thought
In the day and the night,
Both waking and sleeping,
Thy presence my light.

Be thou my wisdom,
Be thou my true word,
Be thou ever with me,
And I with thee, Lord;
Be thou my great Father,
And I thy true son;
Be thou in me dwelling,
And I with thee one.

EIGHTH-CENTURY IRISH,
TRANSLATED BY MARY BYRNE AND ELEANOR HULL

As the hand is made for holding
And the eye for seeing,
You have fashioned me, O Lord, for joy.
Share with me the vision
To find that joy everywhere:
In the wild violet's beauty,
In the lark's melody,
In the face of a steadfast man,
In a child's smile,
In a mother's love,
In the purity of Jesus.

✠ ✠ ✠

There is a mother's heart
in the heart of God.

✠✠✠

Empty and bereft I be;
I cry to thee;
Mother me.

Angry and afraid I be;
I long for thee;
Father me.

Slighted and alone I be;
I reach for thee;
Stay by me.

Thwarted and cast down I be;
I turn to thee;
Hearten me.

Abandoned and forlorn I be;
I run to thee;
Rescue me.

Grieving and in pain I be;
You come to me,
Explain to me;

You feel for me;
You weep for me;
Redeeming me;
Releasing me.

JOYCE DENHAM

THE TRUTH

May the everlasting Father himself
Take you in his own generous clasp,
In his own generous arm.

✠ ✠ ✠

As the rain hides the stars,
As the autumn mist hides the hills,
As the clouds veil the blue of the sky,
So the dark happenings of my lot
Hide the shining of your face from me.
Yet, if I may hold your hand in the darkness,
It is enough, since I know that,
Though I may stumble in my going,
You do not fall.

FROM CARMINA GADELICA,
TRANSLATED BY ALISTAIR MACLEAN

O Christ, you calm the storm at sea;
In tempest sore, be calming me.

O Christ, you walk upon the wave;
When sinking fast, my footing save.

O Christ, the stricken child you raise;
My spirit lift in joy and praise.

O Christ, you heal the man born blind;
Make bright the darkness in my mind.

O Christ, you feed the crowd with bread;
With words of truth let me be fed.

O Christ, you make the water wine;
Take humble gifts and make them fine.

O Christ, the Resurrection Morn,
With your new life, my life adorn.

JOYCE DENHAM

17

I am weary, weak and cold,
I am weary of travelling land and sea,
I am weary of traversing moorland and billow,
Grant me peace in the nearness
Of thy repose this night.

✠✠✠

May the Light of lights come
To my dark heart from thy place;
May the Spirit's wisdom come
To my heart's tablet from my Saviour.
Be the peace of the Spirit mine this night,
Be the peace of the Son mine this night,
Be the peace of the Father mine this night,
The peace of all peace be mine this night,
Each morning and evening of my life.

✠ ✠ ✠

God be with you in every pass,
Jesus be with you on every hill,
Spirit be with you on every stream,
Headland and ridge and lawn;
Each sea and land, each moor and meadow,
Each lying down, each rising up,
In the trough of the waves,
On the crest of the billows,
Each step of the journey you go.

✠✠✠

Though the dawn breaks cheerless
on this isle today,
My spirit walks upon a path of light.
For I know my greatness.
Thou hast built me a throne within thy heart.
I dwell safely within the circle of thy care.

✠ ✠ ✠

THE LIFE

My Christ! my Christ!
My shield, my encircler,
Each day, each night,
Each light, each dark;

My Christ! my Christ!
My shield, my encircler,
Each day, each night,
Each light, each dark.
Be near me, uphold me,
My treasure, my triumph,
In my lying, in my standing,
In my watching, in my sleeping.

FROM CARMINA GADELICA,
TRANSLATED BY ALISTAIR MACLEAN

Hear;
Hold;
Love;
Enfold;
God of all hearing;
God of all holding;
God of all loving;
God all enfolding;

Above the winds, hear me;
Upon the sea, hold me;
On lonely isle, love me;
In dark night, enfold me.

JOYCE DENHAM

O God, who broughtest me
From the rest of last night
Unto the joyous light of this day,
Be thou bringing me
From the new light of this day
Unto the guiding light of eternity.
O! from the new light of this day
Unto the guiding light of eternity.

✠✠✠

My dearest Lord,
Be thou a bright flame before me,
Be thou a guiding star above me,
Be thou a smooth path beneath me,
Be thou a kindly shepherd behind me,
Today and for evermore.

St Columba of Iona

Bless to me, O God,
The earth beneath my foot;
Bless to me, O God,
The path whereon I go;
Bless to me, O God,
The thing of my desire;
Thou Evermore of evermore,
Bless thou to me my rest.

✠ ✠ ✠

Let the flowers close and the stars appear,
Let hearts be glad and minds be calm
And let God's people say Amen.
Amen.

CREATION LITURGY,
THE IONA COMMUNITY

Track Titles

1 The Way

2 The Lark's Melody

3 A Mother's Heart

4 The Truth

5 New Life

6 Peace of the Spirit

7 Circle of Thy Care

8 The Life

9 Hear; Hold; Love; Enfold

10 Today and for Evermore